Hello, my friends! What a great day for school! Our teacher is about to pair us up so we can work together on a super-cool project for the upcoming Science Fair.

_____
This book belongs to:

Text and illustrations Copyright © 2021 by Ocean Aire Productions, Inc. & Sarah B. Tucker

All rights reserved. No part of this book may be reproduced, scanned, or distributed in any printed or electronic form without permission. Please do not participate in or encourage piracy of copyrighted materials in violations of the author's rights.

Library of Congress Control Number: 2023916193

To reach Ocean Aire Productions, Inc. visit: www.AdventuresofHarryandFriends.com

This is a Black Belt Principles Series: Book Eight
Created & Written by Sarah Beliza Tucker - Illustrated by Adam Ihle

ISBN Hardcover: 978-1-953979-21-6
ISBN Paperback: 978-1-953979-20-9
ISBN Digital: 978-1-953979-22-3

It's going to be awesome, especially if my best friend Curly and I get to work together as partners - fingers crossed!

Let's go and find out who our match will be!

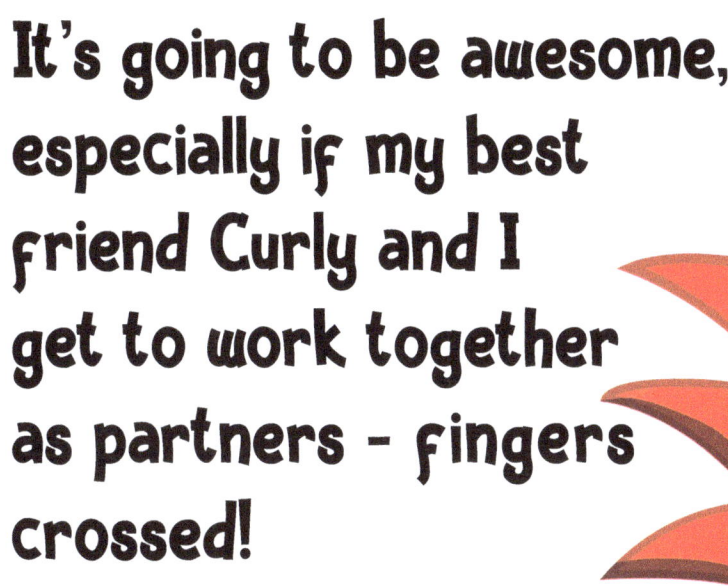

Harry walks calmly into Mrs. Wolf's classroom, ready to find out who his Science Fair partner will be!

Everyone's abuzz with excitement as they spot the phrase "Two Weeks Until The Science Fair!" written boldly on the board - except for Ringo, who, as usual, is messing around.

"Good morning, class!" Mrs. Wolf says with a twinkle in her eye.

"Good morning, Mrs. Wolf!" The class answers in unison as they eagerly take their seats.

"Last week we spoke briefly about our school's upcoming science fair – but get this," she whispers, "I just learned that the top three teams will now have the chance to compete at the STATE LEVEL."

With a loud burst of excitement, she announces, "with judges from your favorite TV show, 'The Adventures of Captain Karate Man!' Talk about a fantastic opportunity!"

The sound of silence fills the room...

"Okay. Okay...Listen up!" Mrs. Wolf announces as she points to the basket she is holding. "I will draw your names from here to create the teams - so pay attention!" She chuckles and then continues.

"Team One: Delilah and Harry." Delilah smiles and glances at Harry, who blushes shyly.

"Team Two: Kara and Honey." The duo cheer enthusiastically.

"Team Three: Ringo and Curly." The two exchange a look of disappointment and dismay.

"Just great. I'll never win now," Ringo mutters as Mrs. Wolf finishes creating the teams.

"Mrs. Wolf... Mrs. Wooolf!"

Curly desperately shouts, frantically waving his hand to get her attention.

Mrs. Wolf approaches Curly's desk, her arms crossed firmly across her chest, and with a slight hint of frustration in her voice, she sighs, "Yes, Curly?"

"There's no way we can be partners!" Curly says, pointing at Ringo.

"Really...And may I ask why exactly?" She asks.

"We don't work well together!" Ringo interrupts.

"Well, boys...This is what we call a learning opportunity." She answers them.

"But... Mrs. Woooolf," they grumble as she walks back to her desk.

"Alrighty, class. Go to your science fair partner and let the BRAINSTORMING begin!" Mrs. Wolf says with a bounce, "Write down as many ideas as you can, and remember, teamwork makes the dream work."

She winks, and the class erupts into conversations. All the kids are excited except for Ringo and Curly, who are now sulking.

While others dream of a volcano erupting or traveling to space,

Ringo and Curly sit, sigh, roll their eyes, and wait for lunch.

As lunch time approaches, Mrs. Wolf strolls up to Ringo and Curly and asks, "How's your project coming?"

"It's not," Ringo replies as the lunch bell chimes.

"I don't understand. You two have had all morning to come up with something, and now it's time to go to lunch," she tells them as the others line up at the door.

Curly starts to respond, "I tried, Mrs. Wolf. It's just...Ringo..."

"Ringo…What? It's your fault, too. Curly!" He snarls.

"You two will now have to work on this after school in the library." She pauses, takes a breath, and says, "I'd like to see three ideas by tomorrow. Now get ready for lunch."

Curly sighs, "Yes, Mrs. Wolf," then continues, "we'll meet at the library after school."

"Good luck with that," Ringo laughs, hops out of his chair, and joins the line.

That evening at their martial arts school, Curly angrily approaches Ringo, unaware that Instructor Dan is listening in.

"Ringo! Where were you?" Curly asks in a demanding tone.

"What do you mean?" He responds.

"I waited for an hour at the library for you!" Curly tells him.

"Oh, that. What's the point? We aren't going to win. So why try?" Ringo shrugs.

"Ummm...because we have to. It's mandatory," Curly answers him.

"What is mandatory?" Ringo asks.

Curly gets frustrated and responds, "It means we have to do the science fair project TOGETHER, no matter what! We only have two weeks to get it done."

"How can I work with you? You're unbearable!" Ringo snaps.

"Me...?" Curly laughs, "Now that's funny." He snaps back.

Quietly, Instructor Dan comes up from behind the boys, startles them, and states loudly, "Oh, boy! You two are like oil and water. It's time to mix things up and teach you a lesson in teamwork." He pauses, then says, "I think for today, instead of Instructor Tom and I throwing for the dodgeball game, you two will."

"Okay. Your job is to work together, as a team, to get everyone out, including Instructor Tom and me." He smiles, then gets serious, "Now...here is the important part, boys: stay on opposite sides of the mat when throwing the ball. Aim below everyone's heads and try not to throw too hard. Safety first, okay?" The boys nod. "Fantastic! As soon as you throw the ball, the game will begin. Let's go play!"

"Why does he get to start with the ball?" Ringo complains loudly from the other side of the mat.

Curly, not having the patience for Ringo's whining, yells out, "Here! You want it. Take it!" and throws the ball as hard as he can in frustration - and it lands right at Ringo's feet.

And so the game begins.

Minutes drag on as Curly and Ringo toss the ball back and forth. They bicker over each missed throw, blaming one another. Suddenly, Curly shouts, "TIME OUT!" and runs to Ringo.

"Ringo...this isn't working. We need to work together."

"Okay...but how?"

"Here's an idea..." he leans in and whispers his plan.

Ringo laughs, "I like it. Let's do it."

Curly quickly returns to the other side of the mat, pretending he has the ball.

The others giggle and run toward Ringo, unaware of what he has hidden behind his back.

Curly winds up and pretends to throw the ball into the crowd as Ringo launches the real one at Instructor Tom's back. It hits, then ricochets off, striking Delilah's shell.

Ringo celebrates as the ball bounces back to Curly, "Yes! Got TWO!"

"Great job!" Curly cheers. The others scatter, trying to avoid being hit, but no such luck.

"See what happens when you work together?" Instructor Dan says, giving the boys a high-five.

"Yes. It was awesome!" Curly responds.

Ringo cheers, "We won!"

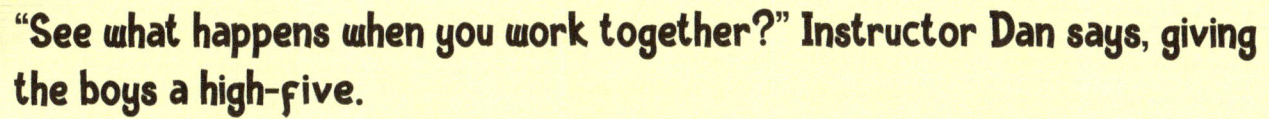

"Yes, you did, Ringo," Instructor Dan chuckles, "all because you two put your differences aside and started to work together. He pauses and then asks, "So the question is now, are you two up for the challenge of the science fair? Can you work as a team?"

"I can now," Curly answers.

"Me too!" Ringo replies. "Me too!"

"Great!" He smiles. "Let's get to class."

"Yes, Sir!" they respond.

Over the next few days, Ringo and Curly meet up after school to attempt to find the perfect science project...

...but after one too many duds...

"Good morning, boys," Mrs. Wolf says as she walks up to their exhibit. "This is Dr. Jones and Dr. Cooper. Can you tell us about your project?"

"We sure can!" They respond together, grinning from ear to ear.

"We came up with this idea after so many other experiments failed. We were even attacked by a bubble monster!" Curly starts to explain...The judges' eyes grow large in anticipation.

"Yes, and after we cleaned up most of the suds, we remembered what our martial arts instructor told us." Ringo interrupts, "He said we were just like oil and water."

"What?" Dr. Jones asks.

"It's because we don't always work well together," Curly tells her.

"But sometimes we do. Just like oil and water, we have one thing that binds us together and unites our competitive spirits into one!" Ringo chimes in.

"Let us show you," Curly says. "We chose to show these four experiments instead of one…"

"to mix things up." Ringo jokes while doing a little dance and stirs the first container of oil and water.

Curly explains, "Our first experiment showed us that no matter how much we stirred, mixed, or shook the mixture..."

"Quite fiercely, I may add," Ringo interjects.

"...they still separated." Curly continues, ignoring Ringo, "We found that the oil was lighter than water and would always rise to the top."

"Like me!" Ringo jests again.

"For our second and third experiment, we combined different elements, like food coloring and a fizz tablet, into the oil and water to see how they would react," Curly shows them.

"We called these two experiments Fireworks and The Red Hot Lava Lamp!" Ringo yells out with excitement, "It really looked cool!"

"But in the end, the oil and water would separate again," Ringo whispers, "Nothing we did or added to it combined the oil and water."

"We were overwhelmed," Curly tells them.

"And I wanted to quit!" Ringo groans.

"So...we started to clean up and brainstorm again...when suddenly, Ringo slipped on the soap suds we forgot to wipe up and spilled an entire beaker of oil and water everywhere!"

"That's when I noticed something cool!"

"What was that?" asks Dr. Jones.

"The answer to combining oil and water," Ringo tells them.

"We learned that the smallest amount of soap helps blend the oil with the water. See..." Curly says as Ringo drops a few drops into the beaker. They all watch as the oil disappears.

"Nicely done, boys. Tell us, what was the one element that bonded you two together?" Dr. Cooper asks.

The boys laugh, "Oh...We like to win."

The Judges nod, scribble down a few notes and move on to the next exhibit.

Moments later, the students all gather around the gymnasium's stage.

"I must say, I am proud of all of you!" Mrs. Wolf tells the students, "Our judges had a hard time picking the top three teams that will move on to the next round."

The students CHEER as she continues, "Winning teams, when you hear your names, please join me here on the stage." She opens the envelope and reads, "Third place is going to the Raging Volcano by Team Delilah and Harry!"

Delilah squeals with joy and hugs Harry, as she jumps up and down!

"Second place goes to The Out of This World Solar System Team by Kara and Honey!" The students continue to cheer as the winning teams make their way up to the stage. "And finally, for our first place team, which I am especially proud of..." She smiles and takes another deep breath.

Ringo and Curly lean in to hear better as the others around them cheer wildly.

"Congratulations...to The Clash of the Titans, by Team Ringo and Curly!" she announces.

After hearing their names, they rush to the stage, high-fiving their classmates as they make their way through the crowd.

On the Stage, Ringo and Curly accept the larger-than-life trophy with the other winners cheering in the background.

"Any words of wisdom you two would like to share with your classmates?" Mrs. Wolf asks them.

Holding their trophy up high! They shout out in unison, "It's all about **TEAMWORK!**"

This fantastic adventure with my friends Curly and Ringo isn't over yet...

Scan the QR code below and download the top 3 science projects to try at home or in your classroom. Remember - let us know how your experiments turn out. We can't wait to hear all about it!

 Scan the QR code to visit our site and check out all of our adventures.

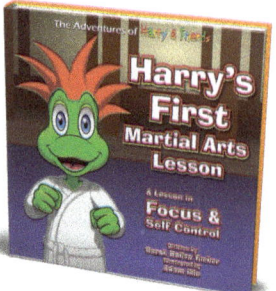
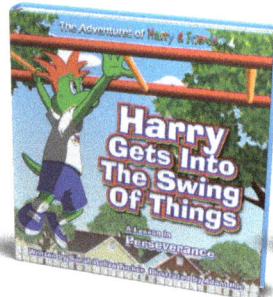
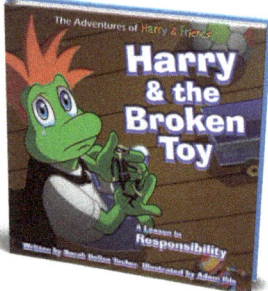
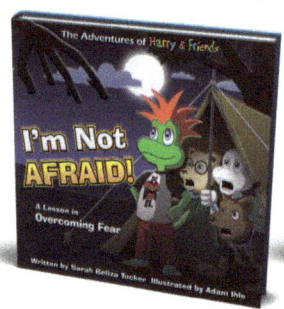
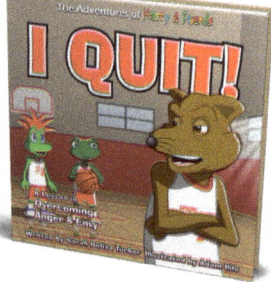

www.ingramcontent.com/pod-product-compliance
Lightning Source LLC
Chambersburg PA
CBHW061349010526
44107CB00011B/877